IMAGES
*of America*

# YELLOWSTONE
# NATIONAL PARK

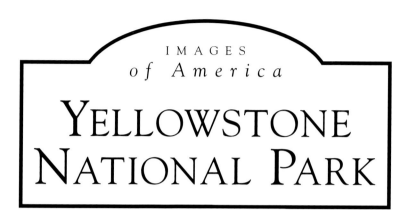

IMAGES
*of America*

# YELLOWSTONE
# NATIONAL PARK

Lee H. Whittlesey and Elizabeth A. Watry

ARCADIA
PUBLISHING

Published by Arcadia Publishing
Charleston, South Carolina

Printed in the United States of America

Library of Congress Catalog Card Number: 2007937565

For all general information contact Arcadia Publishing at:
Telephone 843-853-2070
Fax 843-853-0044
E-mail sales@arcadiapublishing.com
For customer service and orders:
Toll-Free 1-888-313-2665

Visit us on the Internet at www.arcadiapublishing.com

*This book is dedicated to our parents—Charles and Dorothy Whittlesey, Robert and Dawn Lewry—who brought us to Yellowstone as children and instilled a love of the place in both of us. Little did they or we know at the time that the magic of "Wonderland" would captivate our hearts and souls and thus become our life's passion.*

# CONTENTS

# ACKNOWLEDGMENTS

Photographing Yellowstone began in 1871, and many people have been involved in it. We owe debts to early photographers, such as W. H. Jackson and H. B. Calfee. We used many collections to assemble this book. We thank the Yellowstone National Park (YNP) Archives, University of Wyoming, University of Utah, Montana Historical Society, Yale University, Library of Congress, U.S. Geological Survey (USGS), and many private collections.

# INTRODUCTION

For hundreds of years, the area that is now Yellowstone National Park was home to at least 26 Native American tribes. Those tribes, including the "big four" who lived in the area most recently—the Crows, Shoshones, Bannocks, and Blackfeet—called Yellowstone home until 1871, when they were asked to leave in order to satisfy nervous park officials who feared that Native Americans would decrease white tourism. The new park soon became the first incentive for tourist travel to the American West following the Civil War, and its hotels, tent camps, restaurants, stagecoaches, souvenir shops, and tour guides followed quickly as standard parts of the elegant "Grand Tour."

But for most people, the first views of Yellowstone came from photographs. Photography held great power to explain and therefore to transform perceptions of the West from a mythical realm to a place that could actually be visited. Early images became repositories of cultural meanings that subsequent historians and interpreters could decipher.

Initially the photographs were commercial, because members of the ordinary public would not be able to take their own pictures until the 1890s. The commercial photographers came to Yellowstone in 1871. They were men like William Henry Jackson, Joshua Crissman, and Henry Bird Calfee, who used a cumbersome wet plate process that required carrying a great deal of equipment into the wilderness on pack mules. Many of their early images were stereo views—double-image photo cards that could be viewed through a stereoscope to give the viewer a three-dimensional effect. These "touring" images became parlor entertainment for thousands of Americans who before 1920 were without radio, television, or movies. One could be catapulted to far-away lands merely by looking at stereo photographs through a viewer, and this is how thousands of Americans initially "visited" Yellowstone.

World famous since shortly after it was established in 1872, Yellowstone is now a pilgrimage site for visitors from all over the globe. Like Washington, D.C., and Niagara Falls, every American longs to see it at least once in a lifetime. That it was similar as early as 1885 was attested to by tour guide G. L. Henderson, who effervesced about it:

"Nearly 4,000 square miles have been set apart and consecrated to the highest human uses. Every railroad aims to be the medium by which to reach it. Every American must see it once before he dies. All the world dreams of it and reads about it. The best artists photograph it, copy it, and paint it. Men renew their youth in it and women become more beautiful from having breathed its air and inhaled the perfume of its flowers. Boys become wiser and girls lovelier for having visited Fairyland."

Indeed, Yellowstone became known early as "Fairyland" and "Wonderland" from the massive numbers of unique and beautiful individual, natural features: geysers, hot springs, mud pots, steam vents, mountains, lakes, rivers, creeks, waterfalls, canyons, and even petrified trees. So many of these were found that, as early as 1881, photographers like Henry B. Calfee and F. Jay Haynes gave up trying to photograph them all, and today souvenir experts know Yellowstone as the place that boasts the largest number of individual picture-postcard views—more than 10,000. By the time the U.S. Army arrived in 1886 to take care of the place, the park was a vast tourist success.

Served until 1917 by stagecoaches, the park welcomed the automobile nearly simultaneously with the new rangers of the National Park Service, and together they "paved the way" into the 20th century. One million visitors came to Yellowstone in 1948, two million in 1963, and three million in 1993.

Originally the new National Park Service (NPS) believed that parks like Yellowstone needed promotion, and it promoted them feverishly, hoping to increase visitation to the parks and to gain wide approval for the new government agency. By the 1930s, the NPS came to realize that it had done its job well, for promotion was no longer necessary. A Great Depression and a world war allowed Yellowstone to fall into disrepair, but postwar visitation boomed to make the NPS pledge new monies for repair in the massive fix-up known as "Mission 66." Parks certainly needed no further promotion by that time, for during the 1950s, magazine articles began appearing that announced that national parks like Yellowstone were being "loved to death."

Later decades brought their own changes to Yellowstone, as the National Park Service fine-tuned its management. It embraced a "keep it natural" philosophy in the 1960s, weaned bears off their human-food diets in the 1970s, reaffirmed the natural fire policy in the 1980s, and reintroduced wolves in the 1990s. Today the park has truly entered its resource restoration period.

Yellowstone's cultural features—historic buildings, bridges, sites, landmarks, and cultural landscapes and its indoor museum artifacts, photographs, souvenirs, and rare documents—are as interesting as its natural features, but they are less known. One of the purposes of this book is to showcase those features in photographs while still including some natural features. We chose the photographs for their rarity, their unusual portrayal of subjects, their illustrative significance in showing off the place, and their entertainment value. Many of these photographs portray activities that are no longer permitted in the park, such as climbing on or wading in geysers and hot springs, walking off-trail in thermal areas, collecting natural or historic objects, coating specimens with hot spring deposits, picking flowers, cutting trees, and feeding or molesting animals. The National Park Service today asks us not to do those things. This "preservation policy" is part of the park's "keep it natural" philosophy in order to preserve and protect Yellowstone for future generations.

Today Yellowstone's fame, beauty, biology, geology, and antiquity have made it both a world heritage site and a world biosphere preserve. But this book is not the usual printed glorification of elk, bison, bears, and geysers in colorful photographs. Instead it is a celebration of the park's culture and past—the people, places, events, and objects that caused Yellowstone to become the place that it is today. We hope that you enjoy it, and even as you marvel at some of these little-known images, please consider helping us protect Yellowstone so that your great-grandchildren can see it, too.

# One

# EXPLORERS AND
# ESTABLISHMENT
## 1869–1879

Before 1869, white knowledge of the Yellowstone region was almost nonexistent. American Indians inhabited the upper Yellowstone country for hundreds of years without Euro-Americans. Although fur trappers explored Yellowstone's wilderness during the period 1822–1840 and told stories of it, the knowledge they gained of it did not become permanent. During the 1860s, gold prospectors from Montana Territory combed every valley of the future park in the search for precious metal, but they too did not leave lasting information about the area.

It remained for white explorers during the period 1869–1871 to formally reveal the region to the rest of the world. That it required three expeditions to fully reveal the area is a tribute to the richness and complexity of the wonders of the upper Yellowstone. Having heard rumors of strange curiosities at the head of Yellowstone River from fellow prospectors, the Folsom Party, consisting of three men and their pack string, rode through the future park for pleasure in the summer of 1869. They did not publish their account right away but did provide a map, a suggestion to preserve the area somehow, and verbal information to Helena businessmen, who became the next party to explore Yellowstone. That group—the Washburn Expedition of 1870—received ultimate credit for the white discovery of the region. Its leading spirits—Nathaniel Langford, Henry Washburn, and Gustavus Doane—wrote and published accounts of their trip, gave speeches promoting the wonders, drew improved maps, and championed the route for the benefit of the Northern Pacific Railroad. A man in the audience at one of Langford's speeches—Dr. F. V. Hayden of the government's geological survey—appears to have been inspired by it. Or perhaps he was already intending to explore the same country. Whatever the origin of his plans, Hayden obtained $40,000 from Congress the following summer and used it to take some 30 scientists, packers, and cooks into the wilderness to see the Yellowstone wonders. Hayden produced detailed reports and maps, and his photographer, W. H. Jackson, further documented the wonders with his camera. Upon this base of knowledge, Congress passed the law making Yellowstone the world's first national park.

C. W. Cook

While employed by the Boulder Ditch Company in Diamond City, Montana, with David E. Folsom and William Peterson, Charles W. Cook (left) became intrigued with the idea of organizing an expedition to the region in 1868. Cook, Folsom, and Peterson signed on with a group of citizens to explore the region in 1869. When the group dissolved because of the lack of a military escort, the trio decided to make the trip regardless. Upon their return, their attempts to publish their findings found only skepticism by magazines such as *Scribner's Monthly*. Cook worked with Walter Delacy, a previous viewer of Yellowstone's wonders, to produce a detailing their route. This map (below), in addition to Cook's finally published article in the *Western Monthly*, were catalysts for the 1870 Yellowstone expedition by the Washburn party. (YNP Archives.)

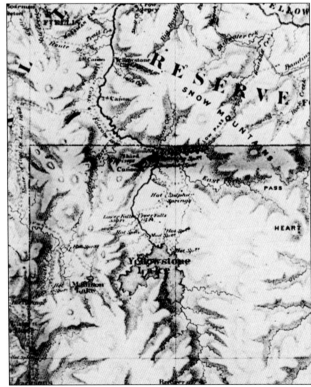

Nathaniel P. Langford (below), bank examiner for Montana Territory, became one of the writers of the 1870 expedition headed by Henry Dana Washburn. Washburn, then surveyor general of Montana Territory, engaged Lt. Gustavus Doane as military escort, and Doane produced the party's official report. Langford's article in *Scribner's Monthly* confirmed the wonders of the Yellowstone region to the world. Unlike Cook's article, Langford's contained images, for *Scribner's* hired artist Thomas Moran to create those images based only on Langford's descriptions. This expedition named natural features, produced another map, and stimulated party members into giving speeches and writing more articles. Langford pushed the idea of making Yellowstone into a tourist attraction for the Northern Pacific Railroad. Eventually the Department of Interior appointed Langford the park's first superintendent in 1872. (YNP Archives.)

SCRIBNER'S MONTHLY.

Vol. II.          MAY, 1871.          No. 1.

THE WONDERS OF THE YELLOWSTONE

meeting with several gentlemen who expressed like curiosity, we determined to make the journey in the months of August and September.

The Yellowstone and Columbia, the first flowing into the Missouri and the last into the Pacific, divided from each other by the Rocky Mountains, have their sources within a few miles of each other. Both rise in the mountains which separate Idaho from the new Territory of Wyoming, but the headwaters of the Yellowstone are only accessible from Montana. The mountains surrounding the basin from which they flow are very lofty, covered with pines, and on the southeastern side present to the traveler a precipitous wall of rock, several thousand feet in height. This barrier prevented Captain Reynolds from visiting the headwaters of the Yellowstone while prosecuting an expedition planned by the Government and placed under his command, for the purpose of exploring that river, in 1859.

The source of the Yellowstone is in a

I HAD indulged, for several years, a great curiosity to see the wonders of the upper valley of the Yellowstone. The stories told by trappers and mountaineers of the natural phenomena of that region were so strange and marvelous that, as long ago as 1866, I first contemplated the possibility of organizing an expedition for the express purpose of exploring it. During the past year,

Vol. II.—1

F. V. Hayden convinced Congress to appropriate $40,000 for a government expedition to Yellowstone in 1871. He hired 30 scientists and a photographer named William Henry Jackson. The group traveled by rail to Corrine, Utah, on the newly constructed Union Pacific Railroad, outfitted there, and traveled north to Montana Territory. This photograph in Red Buttes, Wyoming, of the 1870 Hayden survey contains some of the members who also accompanied the 1871 Yellowstone expedition. (USGS.)

William Henry Jackson is celebrated in the history of the American West as one of its foremost photographers. In 1871, Jackson produced photographs of Yellowstone that helped convince Congress to preserve the region as the world's first national park. He continued to photograph Yellowstone throughout his long life. Like many visual artists of his day, Jackson produced postcards, paintings, and drawings of his beloved West in addition to photography. (NPS, Department of the Interior.)

In this 1878 Jackson photograph, members of a third Hayden survey watched the Old Faithful Geyser erupt. Over time, its interval has shifted from 65 minutes to 95 minutes. But its height and duration have remained the same: 130 feet and 1.5 to 5 minutes. (YNP Archives.)

Old Faithful Geyser is one of the world's most famous natural features. The Washburn Expedition discovered and named this geyser in 1870 because of its regular eruptions. Old Faithful's ornate cone, visible in this 1871 Jackson photograph, was later heavily vandalized. Jackson's photograph taken 20 years later revealed the horrifying damage done to its beautiful, terraced pools by souvenir-hunting tourists. (YNP Archives.)

Artist Thomas Moran immortalized Yellowstone and the Great West in his monumental paintings. His watercolors and paintings portrayed the beauty of the unknown Yellowstone region in such a way as to almost put color into Jackson's photographs. Proclaimed the "Father of the National Parks" in the 1930s, Moran executed the famous painting *Grand Canyon of the Yellowstone*, which now hangs in the Smithsonian. His watercolors and sketches bolstered the lobbying effort to create America's first national park in early 1872. (East Hampton Library.)

Prior to Jackson's photographs of Yellowstone, woodcuts such as this one were the only known images available to a curious public. This woodcut, which appeared in the June 1871 *Scribner's Monthly*, displayed Moran's imagination and artistic ability because he created this illustration of Grotto Geyser sight unseen. (YNP Library.)

Yellowstone's vast territory prompted another Hayden survey in 1872. It built upon the discovery and science of the previous year, and it explored the Grand Tetons. This expedition consisted of two parts: the northern division explored Yellowstone and the southern division explored the Tetons. Jackson took this photograph when the group met in the Lower Geyser Basin. (YNP Archives.)

This exquisite engraving graced Hayden's *Sixth Annual Report* and added flourish and dash to his discoveries. Rendered by an unknown artist who signed the work only with the initials "T. C.," this sensational image of Grotto Geyser, surrounded by other geothermal features, unveiled to the world Yellowstone's dramatic natural wonders. (YNP Library.)

Philetus Walter Norris served as second superintendent of Yellowstone National Park from 1877 to 1882. He is credited with opening up the wilderness of Yellowstone through his road building, his exploring efforts, and his extensive reports, which contributed volumes to the body of scientific and historical knowledge. His achievements in this early era of development are still considered monumental by most historians. (YNP Archives.)

P. W. Norris built and completed the first road between Mammoth and Old Faithful in the summer of 1878. The handwritten caption on this Jackson photograph read: "Entering the Upper Fire Hole Basin, Yellowstone National Park with the first wagon ever there. August 30, 1878." Names of the men written on the photograph were, from right to left, 1) Hibbard, "the scout"; 2) Col. P. W. Norris; 3) Arnholdt; 4) Sturgis; 5) Stoner; 6) Goodwin; 7) Bullock; 8) Burnham; 9) Daily; 10) Burt; 11) Bottler—driver and foreman; 12) Cortman?; 13) Gage; 14) Bradley; 15) Monroe; 16) C'wob?. (YNP Archives.)

James McCartney and Harry Horr built this primitive hostel along with two bathhouses in 1871, attempting to capitalize on hot-water-bathing visitation. Filing a land claim nine days too late on March 10, 1872, McCartney and Horr were declared squatters and eventually evicted from their holdings in Mammoth. (Ole Anderson Collection, Montana State University.)

Shortly after its discovery, Yellowstone became a mecca for commercial photographers. One of the earliest was Joshua Crissman, who plied his trade from 1871 to 1874. He took this stereograph of seven early visitors, two of whom were unidentified women. Walking on formations is prohibited today. (LC-DIG-stereo-1s01154, Library of Congress.)

Commercial photographer John H. Fouch took this photograph of Mammoth in 1878, one of the earliest pictures of civilization there. Other than for McCartney's hostel and bathhouses, the only development at Mammoth at this time was this collection of tents. Only eight of Fouch's Yellowstone photographs are known to survive out of at least 16 that he produced. (Library of Congress.)

Superintendent Norris built this "Blockhouse," the first park administration building, in 1879. Placed atop Capitol Hill because Norris was worried about Native American attacks, the building represented the first real authority in the park. Characterized as run-down, cold, and drafty by 1885, it became what many old park buildings become—employee housing. The blockhouse stood lonely on this hilltop until it was razed one winter day in 1909. (YNP Archives.)

# Two

# DIFFICULTIES, DECISIONS, AND VISIONS

## 1880–1885

During the period 1880–1885, the new Yellowstone Park roiled in turmoil. Railroad tracklayers were attempting to reach the place, a corrupt corporation was attempting to monopolize park land, visitors and employees were illegally hunting animals and destroying delicate geyser formations, civilian officials were incompetent or downright corrupt, and just about everyone was attempting, often without permission, to erect buildings for lodging, housing, sales space, and office space. In short, abuse was rampant, and no one was controlling it. Park officials numbered only around 12. What few regulations were in place had no legal "teeth," and often there was no law preventing a perceived abuse. Police, such that they were, were frightfully few and had no statutory authority. Yellowstone was so geographically remote that Congress had difficulty even learning about the abuses, and the fact that Yellowstone lay in three territories rather than one state did not help matters of jurisdiction and administration.

Thus the stage was set for a period of incredible chaos. Department of the Interior officials fired good-guy Supt. P. W. Norris in early 1882 and replaced him with Patrick Conger. When Conger proved incompetent, the Department of the Interior brought in Robert Carpenter. Carpenter cozied up to corrupt hotel bosses, letting them do whatever they wished, and brazenly staked out park land for himself. Thus the department fired him and hired David Wear. Wear made passable improvements for about a year, but by that time, Congress was fed up with the mess and took a vote to abolish Yellowstone completely. That fortunately failed, but Congress was successful in cutting off all funds to the park. Providentially, Sen. George Vest had attached a rider onto an 1883 law that allowed the Department of the Interior to call on the army during times of difficulty. Beleaguered, the Secretary of the Interior went to the Secretary of War and asked for the U.S. Army to take over Yellowstone. The army marched in on August 17, 1886.

The period had moved from difficulties through controversial decisions to visions by those who wanted Yellowstone protected for the future.

G. L. Henderson (1827–1905) came to Yellowstone in 1882 with his four daughters and one son to be an assistant park superintendent. He moved into this building (left), one of James McCartney's old buildings, that year and made it habitable with his own money. It also served as the post office and was run by his daughter Barbara. Although no one is identifiable here, Henderson's daughters are probably in this photograph. (YNP Archives.)

G. L. Henderson, shown here about 1882, began in the park as an assistant superintendent and became the owner of the Cottage Hotel at Mammoth. From there, he ran his own tours using his own fleet of horses and stagecoaches. Gradually he became the primary Yellowstone lecturer, interpreter, storyteller, and expert. He produced several guidebooks and more than 100 newspaper articles about his time in the park. (Whittlesey collection.)

T. W. Ingersoll captured the building of the National (Mammoth Hot Springs) Hotel in 1883, shown here with scaffolding still on it. Just as important as the hotel is the documentation of Ingersoll's presence in the park at that early date. (YNP Archives.)

Until the publication of this book, historians had not known that Western photographer Carleton Watkins (1829–1916) ever took pictures of Yellowstone National Park. Carleton Watkins photographed the National (Mammoth Hot Springs) Hotel in 1883 with this interesting picture taken from its rear. Other buildings shown in this rare photograph are mostly dwellings or bathhouses. (Yale University.)

D 229 MAMMOTH SPRINGS HOTEL FROM THE TERRACES, NATIONAL PARK.

Another rare, 1883 view of Mammoth Hot Springs by Carleton Watkins, this photograph shows George Wakefield's long transportation building and residence at rear and G. L. Henderson's elongated bathhouse at the front left of the hotel. (Yale University.)

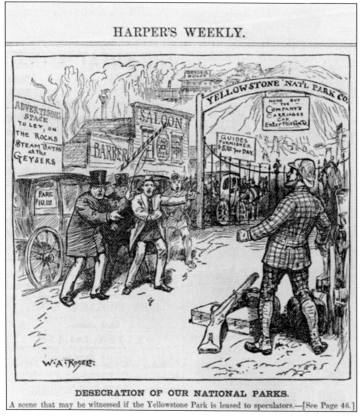

HARPER'S WEEKLY.

DESECRATION OF OUR NATIONAL PARKS.
A scene that may be witnessed if the Yellowstone Park is leased to speculators.—[See Page 46.]

According to this January 20, 1883, *Harper's Weekly* editorial by artist W. A. Rogers, many Americans were not happy with the civilian management of their national park. Speculators swarmed America's newest tourist attraction and applied for leases to build everything from an elevator down to the bottom of Lower Falls to a sanatorium at Soda Butte and thus contributed to Yellowstone's era of difficulties, decisions, and visions. (Library of Congress.)

The Northern Pacific Railroad laid tracks across the plains of Montana, arriving at Livingston in the fall of 1882. Almost immediately, the railroad continued laying tracks south to the national park. The park's first passenger train arrived in September 1883 at a fledgling town named Cinnabar. This photograph shows the depot and platform at Cinnabar, Yellowstone's terminus for 20 years. (Robert Goss collection.)

The Minnesota *Freeborn County Standard* reported on June 3, 1885, "The Railroad Conductors convention at Minneapolis and St. Paul this week, is attended by nearly two hundred of the 'Punch Brothers.' Banquets, rides, and other pleasurable ceremonies are the order of the occasion." On Friday of that week, the party departed for Yellowstone. F. Jay Haynes recorded the "Conductors Excursion" at Mammoth Hot Springs with this rare photograph. (Yale University.)

In his photograph No. 3536, F. Jay Haynes recorded an assistant, James Parris, photographing a man on Minerva Terrace in 1883. The background shows the developing Mammoth village, including the new National Hotel. Just below National Hotel is the long bathhouse owned by G. L. Henderson. At far left was the Ole Anderson specimen tent and to the right of it was the Henderson house, post office, and barn. Other buildings shown were mostly unknown dwellings. Walking on formations is prohibited today. (YNP Archives.)

This rare T. W. Ingersoll photograph shows G. L. Henderson's bathhouse, built in 1882 or 1883. It was short-lived, for park superintendent David Wear forced Henderson to tear it down in 1885. (Bob Berry collection.)

Ole Anderson (1857–1915) came to Yellowstone in 1883 to enter what he called the "magnesia crystallization business." This meant that he coated horseshoes and other objects with hot-spring limestone and sold them to tourists as "coated specimens." He married Christina Granlund (shown here in their wedding photograph) in 1891, and they remained in the park until 1908. (Robert Goss collection.)

Ole Anderson's first "Coated Specimens" tent (1883) was located here against the hillside where the judge's house is today. By 1888, he had moved it closer to Hymen Terrace so as to be near the "coating" hot springs, but he eventually moved back to his original location when he erected his Specimen House (1896). In this photograph, date unknown, Andy Wald sits at right, Ole Anderson is at center, and the man at left is unidentified. (Doris Whithorn, *Pics and Quotes*.)

In another heretofore unknown Carleton Watkins photograph, coating specimen racks are shown in 1883, gradually being buried by travertine as it builds up. Some coated specimens were never claimed and hence were forever buried under the limestone. This activity is prohibited today. (Yale University.)

A fancy coated specimen—a decorated horseshoe from Ole Anderson's family collection—survived to be photographed in 2004. Such items were made in the park at Mammoth from the 1870s to at least 1906. (Robert Goss collection.)

F. Jay Haynes (1858–1921) was the Northern Pacific Railroad's official photographer by 1881 and came to Yellowstone that year. Enthralled by the landscape, he stayed all of his life. Haynes began the series of guidebooks called the *Haynes Guides* and started the Monida and Yellowstone Stage Company in 1898. He and his son Jack Haynes made up a "Yellowstone dynasty" that lasted 81 years. (Whittlesey collection.)

As early as 1884, visitors and park employees called F. Jay Haynes the official park photographer when he set up this home, studio, and sales shop in front of the National (Mammoth Hot Springs) Hotel. His son Jack took over the business in 1916 and ran it until 1962. (YNP Archives.)

Libby Wakefield (left), daughter of stagecoach operator George Wakefield, was known as the "Belle of Yellowstone" during her family's period in the park, 1883–1892. She and an unidentified friend posed at photographer Frank Haynes's tree, a juniper near his house that he constantly used as a backdrop for photography. Libby married Dr. S. F. Way, one of Wakefield's stagecoach drivers. "Doc" Way trained Yellowstone Park Transportation Company stage drivers and later bus drivers. (YNP Archives.)

Photographer Carleton Watkins creatively captured the beauty of Minerva Terrace and the winsome look of two genteel park tourists in this 1883 photograph at Mammoth Hot Springs. Standing directly on the terraces no longer is permitted. (Yale University.)

Early accommodations in Yellowstone were crude. Thomas Rutter took this, the only known image of the park's second hotel. George Marshall built this first iteration of Marshall's Hotel in 1880 on the west bank of Firehole River at the foot of a knoll where Superintendent Norris's road would emerge a year later. Marshall replaced this building in 1884 with one on the east side of the river. (Bob Berry collection.)

Firehole Hotel (formerly Marshall's) was a bustling place in 1885 when T. W. Ingersoll took this picture of 19 people and three wagons there. "Mounted men dash hither and thither," wrote George Bird Grinnell in 1884 as he described wagons, bedding, tents, and lots of people, all hanging out. The hotel served visitors until 1891, when the Fountain Hotel opened one mile to the east. (Yale University.)

The Yellowstone National Park Improvement Company tent camp at Old Faithful went up in 1883, as did the ones at Canyon, Lake, and Norris. These were the first attempts by a concessioner to offer lodging at locations south of Mammoth. Pres. Chester A. Arthur stayed near or partly on the same site that year, and thus these tents have been identified by some sources as his tents. Probably this photograph has a bit of both. (YNP Archives.)

The Shack Hotel, built in (and shown here in) 1885, was Old Faithful's first real hotel. Roundly condemned by nearly everyone, it served visitors until 1894 when it burned. Traveler Eliza Upham complained in 1892 that "there is no paint or wallpaper on the rooms, and no plastering on the walls, only thick paper tacked onto the laths with large-headed tacks, and we can hear readily conversation in other rooms." (YNP Archives.)

Castle Geyser's ornate, globular incrustations, shown in this 1871 Jackson photograph, disappeared early—victims of souvenir hunters who chiseled them away with shovels, picks, and crowbars, only to wastefully pitch many of them out of their wagons later. Such destructive activities were one of the reasons the U.S. Army was called in to protect the national park in 1886. (USGS.)

Castle Geyser was adored by visitors from the earliest days for its 100-foot eruptions from a spectacular cone that resembled a castle. When compared with the Jackson photograph above, the loss of the geyser's ornate deposits is apparent in this 1880s Ingersoll stereo. Standing on formations is prohibited today. (YNP Archives.)

31

Chinaman Spring was named in 1885 when an enterprising Chinese man built this tent over the spring to use its hot water for his laundry. His venture resulted in a wonderful tall tale told by generations of park tour guides about the hot spring "blowing him to Shanghai" when some of his soap fell into the geyser. Whether the story was true or not, existence of his laundry was responsible for at least three newspaper accounts in the 1880s claiming that four Chinese laundrymen were killed when this hot spring erupted. (Doris Whithorn, *Pics and Quotes*.)

Henry Bird Calfee took this photograph of visitors at Giant Geyser in 1881, just in time for one of the travelers, Wilbur E. Sanders, to mention that his party was in the photograph. He thought there were about 50 people present. Walking on formations is prohibited today. (YNP Archives.)

Photographer T. W. Ingersoll took this photograph of a park assistant superintendent and Ingersoll's own wagon and helper probably in 1884. The erupting geyser in the foreground was Sulphur Spring, then a much-viewed feature because the stage route traversed its location at Crater Hills in Hayden Valley. The geyser was later called Crater Hills Geyser. The park official who guided him is unidentified. (Yale University.)

Early travelers at Canyon had difficulty getting across the ravine of Cascade Creek to reach desirable viewpoints on the north rim of the canyon. Superintendent Norris built this bridge in 1880–1881 to provide such access to the viewpoints and to Norris's favorite place in the park—Crystal Falls and Grotto Pool. Later a slightly different crossing became a huge metal bridge that lasted into the 1930s. (Ingersoll, Yale University.)

This pirated photograph from a stereo view company called The Canvassers is important for showing the original station at Soda Butte built by Supt. Patrick Conger in 1884 for his assistant superintendents. When this photograph was taken, in 1886 or 1887, it was in use as a mail station, for James A. Clark (with his wife and son) is shown in the photograph, and he held a mail contract at that time. (YNP Archives.)

James A. Clark built a cottage at Mammoth in 1883 and then drifted into the business of guiding and transporting tourists through the park. In 1885, he received a lease for a "hotel and outbuildings" but evidently built only a barn and tents. Said the *Livingston Enterprise* in 1885, "Clark's Town is at the foot of Capitol Hill, and contains five houses and a number of tents." Clark sold out in 1888 to the Yellowstone Park Association. (YNP Archives.)

# Three

# CHANGING OF
# THE GUARDS
## 1886–1897

During the period 1886–1897, Yellowstone became protected as the status quo changed dramatically for the better. The U.S. Army took over management of the park, the corrupt hotel company went bankrupt, and corporate officials reorganized it as the Yellowstone Park Association. Law enforcement in the park went from essentially nonexistent to the legislated Lacey Act. Congress appointed Judge Robert Meldrum to preside over the first real court of law.

The U.S. Army entered Yellowstone because of corrupt and incompetent civilian officials and complex administrative difficulties that included poaching, vandalism, and problems with park concessioners. The army was not supposed to stay in Yellowstone for very long, but it remained for 32 years, doing a generally credible and efficient job in the eyes of most historians. Enforcing laws, park soldiers quietly went about making order out of chaos, as they stopped poaching and vandalism, prevented the setting of forest fires, oversaw the hoteliers and other concessioners, and gradually settled into the role of protecting the park, much as later park rangers would do. The bankrupt Yellowstone Park Improvement Company stumbled along through 1884 and 1885, and its officials cried loudly that they were innocent as they were forced out of the park. Hotelier Charles Gibson reorganized the company in 1886 into a financially stable one that tried harder to follow the Department of the Interior's regulations. It erected large hotels in lieu of the old tent camps and hired officials who cared more about serving the public.

Congress passed the Lacey Act in 1894 and appointed Robert Meldrum as the first U.S. commissioner. The law made it a crime to hunt animals and birds in Yellowstone and set prison time and a large fine as punishments. The army enforced the act by placing violators in jail, often after marching them many miles on foot.

This period thus "changed the guards" in Yellowstone, whether those guards were park administrators, park concessioners, or those who enforced and adjudicated park laws.

Here the U.S. Army rode into park headquarters at Mammoth Hot Springs and was greeted by Mammoth residents. Both the occasion and the year of this photograph are unknown, but it must have occurred later than 1886, for the board sidewalk was apparently not in existence then. (YNP Archives.)

Soldiers erected Camp Sheridan at the base of Marble Terrace in 1886 because that was the area resource the army perceived it should protect. These buildings remained until 1915, long past the time that the army completed construction of the later establishment called Fort Yellowstone. Here (around 1895) we see the large house occupied by park superintendent George S. Anderson that was long called "the beehive" because so much activity occurred there. (YNP Archives.)

Fort Yellowstone, shown here in or about 1897, began as a post that held one troop and gradually increased in size to four troops (400 men) in 1910. Tents in the background probably indicate that the army did not have enough housing for its men at the time this photograph was taken. The cannon at left was the "sunset cannon," ceremonially fired each evening at sundown from this point atop Capitol Hill. (YNP Archives.)

Lt. Herbert E. Tutherly stands at left, and the army paymaster is the heavyset gentleman at center. F. Jay Haynes took this photograph in 1886 at the then-new "Golden Gate" bridge. The mounted men were guards for the paymaster, while the woman and boy at right were Tutherly's wife, Maroa, and son George. (Whittlesey collection.)

Here two of G. L. Henderson's drivers chauffeured his "fine Quincy carriages" drawn by horses covered with mosquito netting. Henderson's Cottage Hotel appeared at left rear. He and his son built it in 1885 and sold it to the Yellowstone Park Association (YPA) in 1889. (Whittlesey collection.)

The Cottage Hotel, pictured about 1888, was built in 1885 near the site of the present Mammoth gas station. The hotel was built by G. L. Henderson, his son Walter, and his daughters Barbara, Helen, Jennie, and Mary. It was operated as a hotel until around 1910 and then as a dormitory for park employees until it was torn down in 1964. (YNP Archives.)

At Firehole Hotel in Lower Geyser Basin (formerly Marshall's Hotel), YPA officials built two new cottages in 1887. One of them can be seen at right here, supplemented, as many early park hotels were, with tents. This photograph, taken in 1890, showed the party of Edward Burton McDowell standing at the tents. Firehole Hotel closed after the season of 1891, replaced by the new Fountain Hotel located two miles to the east. (Jeff Selleck collection.)

Edward Burton McDowell's 1890 party took this photograph of three party members at Hygeia Spring at Firehole Hotel in Lower Geyser Basin. The Firehole Hotel main building is at rear while one of the new cottages is at right. Visitors to the hotel bathed in hot waters provided by the spring, which was named for the Greek goddess of health. (Jeff Selleck collection.)

Fountain Hotel, shown here shortly after it opened in 1891, was located just north of today's Fountain Paint Pot. Leather Pool, shown at the bottom of this picture, supplied hot water to the hotel's baths via a pipeline whose trench can be seen running across the meadow. Fountain Hotel served stagecoach visitors to Yellowstone through the summer of 1916. Officials closed it in 1917 and burned the abandoned building in 1927. (Whittlesey collection.)

This garbage dump just north of Fountain Hotel quickly became famous after the hotel opened in 1891 from the great number of bears that frequented it. Hotel bellmen earned extra tips by taking visitors there for bear shows like this one in 1899. Naturalist Ernest Thompson Seton photographed and studied bears here in 1897 and again in 1912 for his book *Wild Animals at Home*. (Watry collection.)

Probably the most famous of bears at Fountain Hotel's garbage dump was this one, photographed with empty tin cans at its feet sometime between 1893 and 1899 by hotel manager E. J. Westlake's son. After the picture's first publication, YPA owner Harry Child placed the bear in the center of three red, white, and blue circles, thus creating the logo or company symbol (below) for both his Yellowstone Park Association and his Yellowstone Park Transportation Company (YPTC). (Montana Historical Society.)

The Yellowstone Park Association's bear logo appeared on hotel stationery as early as 1905, but it may have been used earlier. Stated a 1905 company brochure, "The bear who looks at you so quizzically from the cover of this booklet was a 'Fountain bear.' . . . It has been adopted as an emblem to represent Yellowstone Park." It is still used today. (Robert Goss collection.)

The Yellowstone National Park Improvement Company built this, the first hotel at Canyon, in 1886 at the brink of Upper Falls. The building, shown here in 1889, was a low, ramshackle affair that visitors sometimes complained about. The company replaced it in 1890 with the second Canyon Hotel, located north of the canyon. A third Canyon Hotel came later. (YNP Archives.)

Yellowstone Park Association opened the Lake Hotel (still standing today) in 1891, in a location that was then difficult to reach. A visitor that year acknowledged that Yellowstone Lake was lovely and the hotel new but asked rhetorically, "Was this worth that dreadful ride?" Lake Hotel, shown here in 1896, was remodeled in 1903–1904 using huge, Ionic columns that gave it the Colonial look it enjoys today. (*John L. Stoddard's Lectures.*)

Norris was a place where hotels burned down. Tents served during 1883–1886, and the large hotel built there in late 1886 burned to the ground in 1887. Tents again served until YPA replaced them with this (the second Norris) hotel in 1887. Shown here in 1890, it was largely a lunch station with a few overnight rooms. It burned in 1892, and Larry Mathews managed a third tent-and-wood hotel until 1901, when the fourth Norris hotel opened. (Jeff Selleck collection.)

Larry's Lunch Station—Norris's third hotel—was run by Larry Mathews from 1893 to 1900. Larry combined Irish hospitality with a keen wit that kept visitors laughing so hard that they forgot about the spartan meals and accommodations. "Don't drop food on the kyarpet," Larry would tell patrons of his dirt-floored establishment. Here Larry and daughter Lizzie (rear center) look on as his staff serves a meal to stagecoach visitors in 1896. (*John L. Stoddard's Lectures.*)

"CALAMITY-JANE"

Larry's Lunch Station welcomed many famous visitors, such as former president Benjamin Harrison, Speaker of the House David Henderson, and Apache Chief Geronimo. Here Larry and daughter Lizzie laugh it up with Martha "Calamity Jane" Canary, then living in nearby Livingston, Montana. National lecturer John L. Stoddard, who was present at the same time, took this photograph in 1896. (*John L. Stoddard's Lectures.*)

Geologist Arnold Hague and his staff from the U.S. Geological Survey studied Yellowstone every summer from 1883 to 1902. Here they posed near the present Norris campground on Gibbon River with Larry's Lunch Station in the background one day in the 1890s. (YNP Archives.)

A Northern Pacific Railroad train leaves Cinnabar, Montana, in 1896. Cinnabar was Yellowstone's only railhead until the tracks were extended to Gardiner, Montana, in 1902. Before the 1940s, Yellowstone was a place that most visitors experienced by arriving on trains and riding through the park on stagecoaches or buses. Not until 1946 did most visitors bring their own cars to the park. (Montana Historical Society.)

Cinnabar, Montana, shown here in 1896, was the park's only railhead until 1902. A ghost town today, it lived for only 20 years as a tiny hamlet—population 92 in 1900—where visitors stepped off the train and boarded stagecoaches for the park tour. This photograph, taken by national lecturer Burton Holmes, showed visitors boarding a coach next to a table of park souvenirs that were for sale. (*Burton Holmes Travelogues.*)

Northern Pacific Railroad (NPRR) officials visited Mammoth Hot Springs in 1889. Pres. Henry Villard (first row, third from right with hat on his leg) oversaw the building of the railroad to Yellowstone's north entrance in 1883 but got into trouble over its promotional budget. By 1889, he was back in the park's good graces and could visit the park with fellow officials. Here all but Villard are unidentified. The black man standing at right was probably NPRR's chief porter. (Minnesota Historical Society.)

From 1883 through 1948, the Northern Pacific Railroad spent great sums to advertise Yellowstone, producing brochures and broadsides such as this one from 1889. The NPRR promoted the park as "Wonderland," taking that theme from Lewis Carroll's book *Alice in Wonderland*, which was published just a few years before Yellowstone became a national park in 1872. (*Harper's Magazine Advertiser*, Watry collection.)

*Four*

# CONSTRUCTION, CAMPS, AND CAMARADERIE

## 1898–1909

During this period, the U.S. Army and private operators inside and outside of Yellowstone became sophisticated in dealing with tourists. Park concessioners found their stride in erecting and improving hotels, establishing tent camps, and upgrading stagecoach companies. The government improved necessary and desirable infrastructures in the park. And the private sector outside the park augmented facilities in gateway communities to buttress the improvements inside the park. Park visitors became accustomed to great camaraderie while taking the "Grand Tour" on the stagecoaches of all the various companies.

The Yellowstone Park Association (later the Yellowstone Park Hotel Company) built what would become the world-famous Old Faithful Inn, erected a fourth hotel at Norris, and completely remodeled the Lake Hotel, giving it the Colonial styling that eventually made it famous. The Northern Pacific Railroad extended its tracks from Cinnabar to Gardiner, Montana—thus killing Cinnabar and enhancing Gardiner—and built a handsome depot at Gardiner to welcome visitors. The Union Pacific Railroad extended its tracks north to the park's west entrance. W. W. Wylie, having made his movable tent camps a success in the park, received a two-year permit, incorporated his Wylie Camping Company, and then built six permanent camps throughout the park. Wylie sold out in 1905 to A. W. Miles, who immediately received a 10-year permit and built a camp at what became Roosevelt Lodge. Amos Shaw and L. D. Powell established their Shaw and Powell Camping Company in 1898 with movable camps, and shortly after that time, the Lycan, Bryant, Old Faithful, and Holm camping companies all joined the quest for the park's tourism business. Also in 1898, Frank Haynes inaugurated his Monida and Yellowstone Stagecoach Company, which served visitors to the west entrance on red stagecoaches with names, as contrasted with YPTC's yellow stagecoaches at the north entrance, which carried only numbers. The Yellowstone Park Transportation Company, the largest of the stage operators, served hotel visitors with the seeming multitudes of horses, stagecoaches, and drivers. Wylie, Shaw, and all of the other tent companies ran their own stagecoaches as well as lodging. The U.S. Army erected the Roosevelt Arch at the park's north entrance and increased the buildings at Fort Yellowstone to accommodate 400 men.

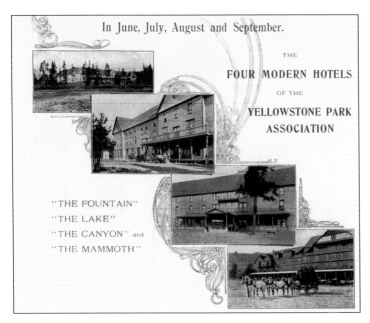

In June, July, August and September.

THE

FOUR MODERN HOTELS

OF THE

YELLOWSTONE PARK
ASSOCIATION

"THE FOUNTAIN"
"THE LAKE"
"THE CANYON" and
"THE MAMMOTH"

Yellowstone Park Association's advertising in the Union Pacific's pamphlet "Where Gush the Geysers" touted four "modern" hotels for the park in 1899. Advertising like this represented (and promoted) the gradual expansion of facilities in the park. Mention of hotels at "Fountain, Lake, Canyon, and Mammoth" did not include a hotel at Old Faithful, as the facility there was crude until Old Faithful Inn opened in 1904. (Watry collection.)

Mammoth Hot Springs Hotel, originally called the "National Hotel," looked like this in or about 1904. Here a six-horse tallyho stagecoach arrived overloaded, as was often the case, and raised dust. (YNP Archives.)

Fountain Hotel (1891–1916) was a busy place when this picture was taken in 1899 by an unidentified party who left us a photo album of their travels. The hotel was situated in an idyllic part of Lower Geyser Basin that took its name from Fountain Geyser. That geyser, which erupted often in the 19th century, also gave its name to nearby Fountain Flats, Fountain Paint Pot, and Fountain Soldier Station. (YNP Archives.)

Lake Hotel, shown here in 1905 after its renovation of the preceding year, reminded some visitors of the White House. Its Ionic, Grecian columns and soft-yellow exterior made it atypical for a wilderness area, but that decor survived through the end of the 20th century and survives today, having sprung from hotels in the East that stood on hills overlooking the ocean. Originally Lake Hotel even sported a widow's walk on its roof. (YNP Archives.)

51

The second Canyon Hotel, photographed here by F. Jay Haynes when brand-new, was first opened for the season of 1890. An unattractive, barn-like structure, it stood just above the site of the third Canyon Hotel and was incorporated into that later building when Robert Reamer built it in the winter of 1910–1911. (YNP Archives.)

This photograph, probably labeled when it was taken on June 5, 1904, captured Canyon Hotel employees on top of a snow bank. The notion that Canyon, at an elevation of over 7,900 feet, could receive snow in June was (then as now) a novel and fascinating thought for many visitors. (YNP Archives.)

This photograph, taken in 1908, was used by the Wylie Camping Company to promote its tent camps in pre-1915 advertising. The location of the camp is today unknown, but the photograph was taken by Harry Shipler of Salt Lake City. (University of Utah.)

The matrons' tent in the Wylie Camp at Swan Lake Flats was immortalized in this 1909 Shipler photograph. A sign on the tree read "Hogan's Alley," saluting the employees' practice of giving names to streets in the camps. The Wylie Camping Company used photographs like these for promotion in advertising brochures. (University of Utah.)

Harry Shipler took this photograph of the interior of the Wylie Camping Company's dining tent at Canyon in 1909. Shipler was a commercial photographer from Salt Lake City whom the company hired to take many camp photographs for use in advertising. (YNP Archives.)

Visitors on the porch of Wylie Hotel, Gardiner, Montana, awaited Wylie's coaches around 1905. W. W. Wylie of the Wylie Camping Company bought the land from the Northern Pacific Railroad in 1903 and built his hotel that same year, for it appeared with photographs of W. A. Hall's then-new 1903 store. (YNP Archives.)

Cinnabar, Montana, was captured here around 1901 in one of the few existing photographs of that tiny hamlet that depicted its buildings close-up. Cinnabar died in 1902 when the NPRR extended its tracks to Gardiner, and an unkindly newspaper writer noted, "Well, thank goodness this blooming town will be wiped off the map when we leave. It's a mystery to me how it ever got on in the first place." But to its residents, Cinnabar was idyllic. (Norman Forsyth photograph, 2003.83.1.16, Gene Autry Museum, Los Angeles.)

Local Gardiner workmen constructed the town's first train depot near the new Roosevelt Arch in 1903. Legend and one historian's undocumented statement have linked the depot with architect Robert Reamer, but that connection is yet unproven. The ornate log train station stood until around 1956, when the Burlington Railroad (successor to Northern Pacific) put up the plain freight station that is the town library today. (YNP Archives.)

In this Underwood stereo view, an NPRR passenger train arrived at Gardiner depot, probably in 1904, while two drivers and their wagons awaited its unloading. Sepulcher Mountain can be seen at rear. (YNP Archives.)

The seldom seen interior of the Gardiner depot was captured here in a c. 1903 photograph, complete with three lounging NPRR employees. (Robert Goss collection.)

This panoramic photograph of a six-horse tallyho stagecoach leaving the Gardiner depot and heading park bound with its "dudes" for the Roosevelt Arch was taken in or about 1904. (Robert Goss.)

Visitors looking through the Roosevelt Arch after Hiram Chittenden built it in 1903 could also see the new Gardiner passenger depot. Chittenden desired the arch because he thought the north entrance to "Wonderland" uninteresting. Pres. Theodore Roosevelt, vacationing in the park in 1903, accepted an invitation by Gardiner businessmen to speak at the dedication, thus setting the stage for Gardiner's big day. (Underwood stereo, YNP Archives.)

Five men who drove the six-horse tallyho stagecoaches for the Yellowstone Park Transportation Company posed for this photograph in 1909 wearing their Stetsons and linen dusters. They were, from left to right, Jack "Johnny" McPherson, John "Daddy" Rash, Al McLaughlin, Harry Lloyd, and Wallie Walker. At least seven other men of this elite cadre are known to have driven the tallyhos. Said another driver, "These men never touched a horse," meaning that they only drove, and others did the messier work for them. (YNP Archives.)

Stagecoaches, like later buses, got dirty and had to be cleaned. This washing facility was located in the transportation yard at Mammoth, where there was also a paint shop, repair shop, blacksmith shop, and many carriage stalls. The photograph is undated but is probably from around 1908. (YNP Archives.)

Stage driver Eugene Truax posed about 1911 in front of the new (third) Canyon Hotel with horses no doubt attached to his coach. He wore a white Stetson and white linen duster, probably with the large yellow buttons that characterized a Yellowstone Park Transportation (YPT) Company driver. (Courtesy descendant Maxine Shuler.)

According to descendant Maxine Shuler, this photograph depicted Eugene Truax driving a six-horse tallyho stagecoach around 1907 on its way to Mammoth. If true, it means that Truax, at least for a time, was one of the elite six-horse drivers for the YPT Company. (Courtesy Maxine Shuler.)

This idyllic photograph captured tourists at Old Faithful Inn with the gnarled bridge over Myriad Creek about 1910. The bridge seemed to have sprung from the book *Alice in Wonderland* and was festooned with strange, mushroom-like wood formations, probably from a burled Yellowstone forest located five miles east of Old Faithful. (Whittlesey collection.)

The lobby of Old Faithful Inn, shown around 1904, has captivated visitors since architect Robert Reamer oversaw its construction in 1903–1904. The chimney contains 500 tons of native rhyolite rock, and viewing this interior is something like looking at the skeletal inside of some primeval dinosaur. (E. W. Kelley stereo, YNP Archives.)

Pres. Theodore Roosevelt vacationed in Yellowstone in 1903, just in time to lay the cornerstone of the Roosevelt Arch at the park's north entrance. Upon arriving here at Cinnabar, Montana, Roosevelt laughed to park superintendent John Pitcher (at his left in this photograph), "Major, I am back in my own country again." (YNP Archives.)

Roosevelt spent a couple of weeks in the park's backcountry in 1903, camping and viewing animals. He looked at the camera, probably held by Supt. John Pitcher, while naturalist John Burroughs (with white beard) stood at Roosevelt's left and guide Elwood "Billy" Hofer sat. The man behind Roosevelt has not been identified. (Library of Congress.)

The Shaw and Powell Camping Company, formally established in 1898, competed with the Wylie Camping Company for visitors who wanted a cheaper way to see and experience Yellowstone. This driver chauffeured what was apparently the company's "chuck" (kitchen) wagon around 1905. (YNP Archives.)

Nationally known female photographer Frances Benjamin Johnson (1854–1952) took this photograph in 1903. Like the early Wylie Camping Company, the Shaw and Powell Company transported visitors around the park, carrying all camping supplies and food with them. Here a tour group enjoyed lunch while employees did the necessary chores. (Library of Congress.)

Following his years at Norris Lunch Station, Larry Mathews was transferred to the Old Faithful Lunch Station. He managed that facility in 1902 and 1903. It looked like this in 1902, complete with wicker benches, when Frances Benjamin Johnson photographed it. Said G. L. Henderson that year, Larry "informed me that one night he had stowed away under the cloth roofs 193 pilgrims and not a growl of discontent had passed any of their lips." (Library of Congress.)

Park bears frequented open-pit garbage dumps in Yellowstone for at least 85 years, until the National Park Service closed the last such dump in 1970. Here tourists watched bears at what was probably either the Canyon or Fountain Hotel dump around 1895. (F. Jay Haynes photograph; Randy Ingersoll collection.)

In early days, there were no boardwalks in park thermal areas, and visitors could walk wherever they wished. This tourist group climbed to the top of what was probably Mound Terrace in or about 1905 to look out at the Mammoth Hot Springs Hotel and village below. Walking on formations is prohibited today. (E. W. Kelley, Presko Binocular Company.)

Beginning in 1884, visitors routinely descended into the Devil's Kitchen, a cave at Mammoth that was the crater of an extinct hot spring, to examine bats and formations. Here a uniformed hotel tour guide sat next to the ladder while his "dudes" examined the cave about 1906. The cave was closed to visitors in 1939. (Published by Berry, Kelley, and Chadwick of Philadelphia; Bob Berry collection.)

This Harry Shipler photograph from 1908 shows visitors at the Wylie Camping Company's Lake camp returning from a fishing trip. In those days, visitors dressed up to travel through the wilderness. As early as 1887, there was a commercial tent camp at Lake, and the Wylie Camping Company established its camp there in 1898. (University of Utah.)

This cone-shaped hot spring was first observed and documented by the 1870 Washburn Expedition as party members watched a fisherman's trout accidentally fall off the hook into the hot spring, and when the fish surfaced, it was literally boiled. Catching fish and cooking them on the hook in Fishing Cone quickly became a feat that enamored many early visitors but is no longer permitted. (YNP Archives.)

From 1898 to 1906, A. F. "Uncle Tom" Richardson ran tours at Canyon, near the trail that today bears his name. Prior to the 1903 building of the bridge to Artist Point, Richardson boated visitors across the river, fed them lunch, and escorted them down into the canyon to the base of Lower Falls via ropes. Here visitors descended in 1904, with Richardson holding the rope at right. (O. W. Dean lantern slide 85, NPS, Harpers Ferry.)

Petrified trees near Tower Junction were interesting to early visitors, and originally there were two such trees there. Here visitors stood on top of one of them around 1900. By 1907, one tree had been completely dismantled by souvenir hunters, so the U.S. Army fenced the other one to protect it. (YNP Archives.)

West Thumb Lunch Station was established by the Yellowstone Park Association in 1892, during the first summer after the Old Faithful–West Thumb road was completed. Near it was the spot where the steamboat *Zillah* docked to ferry passengers to Lake Hotel. In this *c.* 1904 photograph, visitors are shown walking from the station to the boat. (T. W. Ingersoll photograph; Bob Berry collection.)

E. C. Waters established a boat business on Yellowstone Lake in 1896 and eventually wanted a larger boat. In 1905, he built the steamboat *E. C. Waters* at Lake, a boat that he claimed could carry 600 passengers. When the Steamship Navigation Service refused to license it for more than 125 people, Waters abandoned it at Stevenson Island. Here the *Zillah* and the *E. C. Waters* wait at the dock in front of Lake Hotel in 1905. (Barkelow postcard; Watry collection.)

Howard Eaton (1851–1922) established one of the nation's first dude ranches (at Medora, North Dakota, and later at Wolf, Wyoming) and began taking groups of horseback travelers to Yellowstone in 1885. He thus became the park's earliest and longest continuous outfitter, making his last horse trip around Yellowstone not long before he passed away. When he died, the trail that he used for so long was named for him, the Howard Eaton Trail. (YNP Archives.)

Here one of Howard Eaton's horseback groups pauses to be photographed in 1899. This particular group was styled the "H. E. Tough Riders," probably a play on Theodore Roosevelt's Rough Riders of that day. Horse groups got larger and larger in Yellowstone until, in 1927, Dick Randall took the Sierra Club party of 173 people through the park. (YNP Archives.)

THE "H. E." TOUGH RIDERS,
YELLOWSTONE PARK,
AUGUST 1899.

# *Five*

# FACING A NEW ERA
## 1910–1915

During the period 1910–1915, Yellowstone became sophisticated and seasoned in transporting and caring for park visitors who took the "Grand Tour" by stagecoach. The U.S. Army quietly patrolled and protected the national park while hotels and camping companies transported, housed, fed, and entertained tourists. Workmen erected the huge Canyon Hotel in 1910, and the Yellowstone Park Hotel Company opened it in 1911. Old Faithful Inn received a large east wing in 1913, and the Mammoth Hot Springs Hotel was renovated into essentially a different hotel in the same year. The YPT, Monida, Wylie, and Shaw/Powell companies operated stagecoaches in the park. The Bryant, Lycan, Holm, and Old Faithful camping companies joined Wylie and Shaw/Powell to care for visitors who wanted a cheaper way to see Yellowstone. The U.S. Army added a fourth troop to its numbers, such that 400 soldiers took care of the park, and it completed construction on its large complex called Fort Yellowstone.

But discussions of eliminating the army from parks and founding a government agency specifically to manage parks began as early as 1907 and soon became serious. Several conferences on national parks were held during this period wherein discussions ensued as to the usefulness (or not) of the army and the need for (or not) of a new agency to manage the national parks.

Agitation for automobiles also became serious. "Good roads" clubs blossomed around the nation and their members began to call for opening Yellowstone and other parks to automobiles. In 1915, park superintendent Lloyd Brett accompanied Amos Batchelder of the American Auto Association and other officials on a test ride around Yellowstone and, to no one's surprise, reported in favor of the car.

During this period, Yellowstone hovered on the brink of the modern age but had to be dragged, very slowly, into it. The park was essentially the last place in the nation to allow automobiles into its sacred portals, and the new National Park Service was created after nearly a decade of discussions within and outside of Yellowstone.

WHERE GUSH THE
GEYSERS

OREGON SHORT LINE
ALL RAIL ROUTE TO THE
YELLOWSTONE

*Where Gush the Geysers* (above) was a classy pamphlet from the Oregon Short Line Railroad that went into numerous editions between 1899 and 1910. National writer Elbert Hubbard gushed unashamedly that year that "this book is the finest and most satisfying piece of commercial literature ever put out in America, Europe, Asia, or Africa." All of the five railroads that eventually served Yellowstone produced colorful pamphlets promoting the park and the railroads' Western tours. Many of these are collectors' items today, including this 1910 edition with Giant Geyser on its cover. Geysers were more interesting when they were real, as the photograph below shows of Grand Geyser erupting 200 feet tall in 1911. Before 1969, Grand's long, tall bursts numbered anywhere from 6 to 45, but later there were only 1–5 bursts. Intervals have averaged 6–15 hours (often 8 hours). (Watry collection/Library of Congress.)

Henry Brothers got permission from the park to establish his "Geysers Baths" near Old Faithful in 1914 and opened it in 1915. Using hot water from Solitary Geyser, above Geyser Hill, the bathhouse was open through 1933, when Charles Hamilton purchased and remodeled it. Its last season in operation was 1949. (YNP Archives.)

This delightful photograph of Wylie Camping Company visitors posing on the cone of Grotto Geyser was taken around 1910. The Wylie camp at Old Faithful was located on Wylie Hill immediately west of Grotto Geyser, so it was a favorite background for tourists' photographs. Metal signs like this one reading "Grotto" were erected in 1907. (YNP Archives.)

Harry Shipler was a commercial photographer from Salt Lake City who came to the park (1908–1909, 1911–1912, 1915–1916) at the behest of the Wylie Camping Company to photograph Wylie camps for advertising purposes. The Wylie Company ran a promotion in 1914 offering a trip to Yellowstone to anyone who could guess the number of wooden spools in this display case in downtown Salt Lake City. (University of Utah.)

Still more Wylie Camping Company promotional materials were assembled for this collage presented on a postcard in 1912 by Bloom Brothers. There were six different iterations of this postcard, one for each day of the five-day Wylie tour plus a sixth card for the Gardiner portion of the tour. (Watry collection.)

In 1905, W. W. Wylie sold his Wylie Camping Company to A. W. Miles of Livingston, Montana. Miles ran the company through the end of the stagecoach era in 1916. Here Miles posed in a single-horse surrey in 1915 at his Upper Basin Camp on Wylie Hill. (University of Utah.)

This unidentified Wylie Camping Company tour group posed at their stagecoach in 1911 at the Sleepy Hollow lunch station, sometimes called the Gibbon Lunch Station. The latter name was confusing because the rival Shaw and Powell Company also had a Gibbon Lunch Station. (University of Utah.)

The Salt Lake Commercial Club's trip to Yellowstone in August 1912 was captured at the Riverside Camp by photographer Harry Shipler. Containing over 100 people, the group was carried around Yellowstone by the Wylie Camping Company. (University of Utah.)

Wylie Camping Company's dining tents were initially set in a more individual manner, but by the time this photograph was taken in 1911, the eating tents had become plainer and were oriented to mass-production feeding. This facility was at Canyon Camp. (University of Utah.)

The Holm Camping Company, owned by Tex Holm of Cody, Wyoming, competed with Wylie by bringing camping parties from the east across Sylvan Pass. Here a Holm wagon has trouble getting over the pass because of snow in July 1909 as the company was bringing in members of the Geographic Society of Chicago. (Meta Mannhardt photograph, Geographic Society of Chicago.)

The Meta Mannhardt party of 44 from Chicago posed for this photograph at lunch in 1909. Tex Holm himself is at the center of the photograph with the American flag above his head, standing to the left of and behind a man in a white shirt. (Meta Mannhardt photograph, Geographic Society of Chicago.)

The second Mammoth Hot Springs Hotel had a dining room with a somewhat radical, futuristic look to it, unusual for the period in which it existed: 1913–1936. (Library of Congress.)

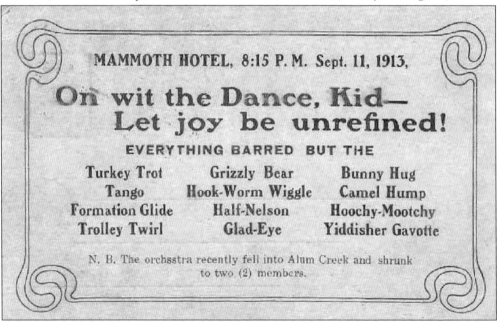

MAMMOTH HOTEL, 8:15 P. M. Sept. 11, 1913,

## On wit the Dance, Kid— Let joy be unrefined!

### EVERYTHING BARRED BUT THE

| | | |
|---|---|---|
| Turkey Trot | Grizzly Bear | Bunny Hug |
| Tango | Hook-Worm Wiggle | Camel Hump |
| Formation Glide | Half-Nelson | Hoochy-Mootchy |
| Trolley Twirl | Glad-Eye | Yiddisher Gavotte |

N. B. The orchsstra recently fell into Alum Creek and shrunk to two (2) members.

Dancing at park hotels began in stagecoach days and continued through the 1950s. This 1913 dance poster guaranteed a good time by implying that almost nothing was forbidden and then listing 12 types of dances that patrons could try. The Alum Creek mention at bottom was a reference to a tall tale told by stage drivers as early as 1896 that the waters of Alum Creek could shrink things. (YNP Archives.)

Joseph Warren Black (1873–1954), the driver of this four-horse coach at the third Canyon Hotel, brought his party of tourists in from Teton, or Tetonia, Idaho, around 1910. The company that Black worked for is indiscernible here, but service from Idaho indicates that it was either the Monida and Yellowstone Company or one of the many independents who operated from outside the park. (YNP Archives.)

Stage driver "Yellowstone Chip" Samuell (1891–1978) here reined his Wylie coach and "four whites" through the Wylie Camping Company's Sleepy Hollow (Gibbon) Lunch Station. The year was either 1913 or 1915 because those were the only two years that Samuell worked for Wylie. Samuell recalled later that one of the two men "on the box" with him here was John D. Rockefeller's personal secretary. (Chip Bowles collection.)

Road engineer Hiram Chittenden built the first iteration of Fishing Bridge in 1902, at the same time he built the park's east entrance road, which was intended to connect with Cody, Wyoming, where the new Chicago, Burlington, and Quincy Railroad had just arrived. The covered wagon seen on the bridge around 1912 was not typical of most park vehicles and was probably operated by a "sagebrusher," that is, a tourist who traveled in his own "outfit." (Stereo Travel Company, Bob Berry collection.)

The road across Dunraven Pass and Mount Washburn, which opened in 1905, was downright dangerous in places. Here a two-horse surrey makes its way across about 1912. (YNP Archives.)

The Upper Geyser Basin Soldier Station at Old Faithful (c. 1916), located on Firehole River just west of Lion Geyser, began from a single cabin built by P. W. Norris in 1879 and lasted until the NPS tore the complex down in 1921. The U.S. Army operated from these stations to protect delicate geyser formations from souvenir hunters. (YNP Archives.)

The Canyon Soldier Station, built in 1898, was located at today's brink-of-Upper-Falls parking area. Like others in the park, it became a ranger station when the army left Yellowstone. This c. 1914 photograph showed the gnarled-wood railings that became popular on footbridges in the park beginning in 1905. (YNP Archives.)

In 1915, the Panama Pacific Exposition (the World's Fair) was held at San Francisco. It featured a huge replica of Old Faithful Inn astride a life-size map of the entire park that visitors could actually walk on. This was the cover of the Union Pacific Railroad's promotional pamphlet about the affair. (Watry collection.)

This 1915 world fair pamphlet proclaimed, "The Exhibit of the Union-Pacific System at the Panama-Pacific Exposition has an educational value quite out of the ordinary, showing . . . in full size some of the noteworthy features of Yellowstone National Park, and, in accurate relief model, the contour of the entire district. An actual geyser and a full-size waterfall are features." (Watry collection.)

Howard Hays's 1914 pamphlet titled "An Appreciation" stated of the exposition's giant replica of Old Faithful Inn, "The dominant feature of the exhibit is Old Faithful Inn, which covers a ground area of 47,000 square feet. . . . The reproduction is exact. The interior is a banquet hall of such gigantic size that 2,000 guests will be seated without crowding. . . . At one end . . . is a concert stage where a symphony orchestra of eighty pieces will [perform]." (Watry collection.)

The Morris party, shown here in front of the Old Faithful Inn in 1913, surely encountered the leisurely pace of Yellowstone's horse-and-buggy tours. Just two years after this photograph, what one historian has called the "best of all possible worlds" came to a close, as those "infernal combustion machines" finally gained entry into the hallowed gates of Yellowstone. (YNP Archives.)

Six weeks before the automobile was allowed into Yellowstone on August 1, 1915, park officials conducted a test run consisting of two automobiles carrying VIPs to see whether cars were feasible in the park. When the two cars arrived at the Upper Basin Wylie Camp on June 7, 1915, they were touted as the first automobiles ever at Old Faithful. The front car carried the five men identified below, while the rear car, a Franklin, carried its owner, L. H. Van Dyck, and his wife and daughter. (YNP Archives.)

Riding in this, the lead car, were Harry Child in the front passenger seat with his son Huntley Child as driver. In the backseat were, from left to right, Amos Fries (road engineer), Col. Lloyd Brett (park superintendent), and Arthur W. Miles (owner of Wylie Camping Company)—all featured here at Old Faithful Inn. Emmett Hood's recent article has corrected the date of this event from August 15, 1915, to June 7, 1915. (YNP Archives.)

*Six*

# ENTER THE AUTO AND THE NATIONAL PARK SERVICE
## 1916–1929

During the period 1916–1929, the U.S. Army was leaving Yellowstone (completed in 1918) and the new National Park Service (NPS) was taking over the park's administration. These developments finally occurred after many years of debates over when and if the army should leave and who should assume command. Simultaneously these two government agencies allowed automobiles into the park after years of debate about that subject.

These two developments were major and changed the park dramatically forever from a quiet place of less than 25,000 visitors to a busy place where everything needed to be larger and visitors numbered more than 200,000. Introduction of the automobile and establishment of the NPS created five years of confusion and chaos as the new agency struggled to merge numerous concessioners into single units, to upgrade park roads for accommodation of automobiles and auto campers, to figure out what the new rangers should do with law enforcement and park interpretation, and to generally learn how to administer not only Yellowstone but also at least 30 other national parks.

Park officials quickly discovered that automobiles and horses could not easily occupy the same roads, that automobiles reached destinations more quickly so many hotels and lunch stations were no longer needed, and that the park road system was too narrow and primitive for cars. Horace Albright assumed the superintendency in 1919 and made great administrative changes. The Yellowstone Park Transportation Company motorized park touring by purchasing over 100 new touring cars called buses. U.S. engineers began major work on park roads. The NPS got rid of numerous old concessioners and created new, singular companies under a "regulated monopoly" system. The new rangers demolished many old structures and built new ones as they began realizing that the old ways of dealing with park resources, such as bears and geysers, did not always work without better science. Yellowstone began to lurch slowly into modernity, not always efficiently and often with "wheezes and groans," in much the same fashion as the new automobile itself.

## THE STAGE DRIVER'S FAREWELL TO THE AUTOMOBILE MAN.

A stage-driver lay asleep by his wagon;
He was one of the old-fashioned school.
He had a big glass jug of whiskey,
And nearly a quart of white mule.
His cuffing sack served for a pillow;
His robes he used for a bed;
And when he awoke from his slumbers,
He rolled him a pill as he said:

All my life I have been a wild savage;
All I know is the tackie and dude;
And I've stemmed them around this old circle
For the last twenty years. Am I rude
When I say you're a misguided pilgrim,
And you're driving me away from my home,
With your sweet-scented gasoline wagon,
So that to foreign lands now I must roam.

I just want to say to you, stranger;
You may be a pretty good scout;
But you motored into this National Park
And chased the old savages out;
And I'll be damned if I ever can like you,
Or pretend that I like your machine,
Or your racket and noise, or the rest of your junk,
Nor the smell of your cheap gasoline.

Farewell, you old wonderland country,
Good-bye to the geysers and falls,
Adios to the bo's and the heaver's,
I am going away from them all,
No more shall I drive the wild pony,
As in the old days gone bye,
And he took a big drink from his bottle,
And brushed a tear from his eye.

Farewell you evergreen mountains,
The fairest green spot on God's earth;
I am going to leave you forever,
Going far from the land of my birth.
But here's luck to all you spark-plug cleaners,
You have gasolined in here at last,
May you have the same luck in the future
I and my tackies have had in the past.

This stagecoach driver's poetic and emotional farewell to the automobile man reads like a eulogy to the passing of a simpler time in Yellowstone. For over 30 years, the horse-and-buggy days of touring the park to these stage-drivers seemed like heaven on earth compared to the fuming, backfiring, and gasoline-smelling days of the automobile era. (Whittlesey collection.)

One of the passengers of these flag-waving cars speeding through Sylvan Pass from Cody, presumably on August 1, 1915, could have been Buffalo Bill. In 1916, park concessionaires continued to transport tourists by stagecoaches with the exception of the Cody-Sylvan Pass Motor Company, which operated auto stages from Cody to Lake Hotel. (YNP Archives.)

Cars were heavier, faster, and sometimes wider than stagecoaches, so Yellowstone's roads became outmoded almost immediately after automobiles were allowed into the park. Heavy cars created huge ruts in the park's dirt roads whenever the roads became wet, as shown here in a 1920s photograph of an automobile in Hayden Valley. (YNP Archives.)

The road up Mount Washburn, which originally went all the way to the top and down the other side, was completed by road engineer Hiram Chittenden and opened in 1905. It was narrow and dangerous, and it remained that way when automobiles began to use it in 1915 and in this photograph in 1924. (YNP Archives.)

Beginning in 1915, when automobiles were first admitted into the park, car camping was immediately in vogue. Here a man and a boy pose in 1924 with their car loaded for camping. Note the large canvas tent stowed on the car's running board along with pots, pans, and other necessaries. (YNP Archives.)

By 1924, there was a formal auto camp at Mammoth, and these folks were camped there with one lady engrossed in her writing table. Interestingly, in those days, campers often placed their cars in the tents and slept outside themselves in an attempt to protect the automobiles' leather seats from rain damage. (YNP Archives.)

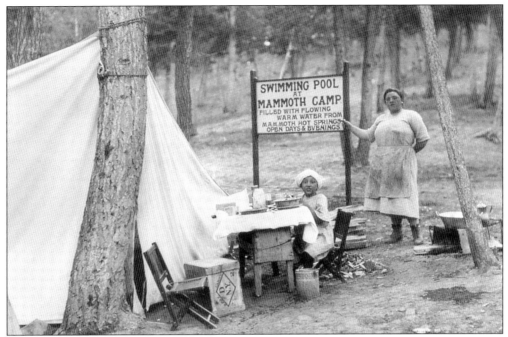

The park's black photo albums include this photograph with the politically incorrect caption "stoutest visitor for 1923." The woman and her son were camped at Mammoth campground when she was photographed pointing to a National Park Service sign advertising the new swimming pool. (YNP Archives.)

In 1920, officials of the Yellowstone Park Camping Company opened a swimming pool near Mammoth Lodge. Here visitors were captured swimming there in the mid-1920s. (YNP Archives.)

The Yellowstone Park Transportation Company purchased 90 of these White Motor Company series B-5, ten-passenger vehicles in the spring of 1925 after a disastrous fire destroyed the beautifully designed 1904 Robert Reamer Transportation building, 75 touring buses, and 18 other cars in March. YPT bus No. 316, pictured here at the Mammoth Hotel, was the "official car" of the Union Pacific Railroad. (YNP Archives.)

Also popular in the 1920s was the practice of having large groups traveling together to Yellowstone. Here the Wasatch Mountain Club from Salt Lake City arrived in Yellowstone in 1923. One of their members, A. M. Simms, left a written account of the trip. Note the canisters on the front of the car, which held acetylene for the car's headlights. (YNP Archives.)

The Canyon Lodge (1924–1956), located where the parking lot for Uncle Tom's Trail is today, had roots in 1913 as a Shaw and Powell tent camp. When the park was motorized in 1917, Yellowstone Park Camping Company took over the site, built the lodge as a main structure, and kept the tent cabins. Here we see the interior of the lodge in or about 1923. (Jack Haynes postcard 23559, YNP Archives.)

Forerunners of present-day NPS campfire programs began in tent camps during the stagecoach days when camping company employees performed skits and poetry readings for tourists. The Wylie Camping Company and the Shaw and Powell Company both presented such nightly programs. As shown here, a huge crowd of around 1,100 people attended a YP Camps Company program in 1923. (Jack Haynes photograph, YNP Archives.)

TOWER FALLS 1918

Bears, which fed at stagecoach-era dumps as early as 1888 if not 1883, began to appear on park roadsides as early as 1910 to ask for handouts. That problem got bigger when the park motorized. Here a black bear "asks" for a handout in 1918 at Roosevelt Camp near Tower Fall. Feeding bears is prohibited today. (George Bowles collection.)

This c. 1921 photograph recorded a black bear standing upright to "ask" for food in the park. Feeding bears is prohibited today. (YNP Archives.)

This porte cochere (overhang) that is long gone today was built in the 1920s at Lake Hotel to shelter automobiles like these. (YNP Archives.)

The third Canyon Hotel (1911–1958) hosted stagecoaches and then automobiles. Here visitors surround their cars sometime between 1917 and 1924. The occasion is unknown. (YNP archives.)

In 1924, store owners Anna Pryor and Elizabeth Trischman erected a snack shop on the upper terraces near the cave known as the Devil's Kitchen. They styled their new enterprise, shown here in 1929, the Devil's Kitchenette. It was a short-lived business that lasted only through the mid-1930s. (YNP Archives.)

These exquisitely dressed visitors seemed delighted to witness what were, according to explorer Capt. John Barlow, the beautiful "curbing of rock" and the "silicate scallops" of Punch Bowl Spring in the 1920s. An 1880s Ingersoll photograph labeled the spring "Fairies Well," and the Wylie Camping Company piped the waters of this dish-shaped spring to supply its nearby tent camp. Walking on formations is prohibited today. (YNP Archives.)

By the 1920s, Uncle Tom's Trail, which was built in 1905 and descended into the canyon below Lower Falls, was a great tourist success. As shown here, visitors in the 1920s enjoyed it in large numbers. (George Bowles collection.)

Handkerchief Pool became one of the park's most famous hot springs during the period from 1888 to 1926, when it was known for being the spot where one could watch one's handkerchief be sucked down and then spit back up. The subject of a 1913 study in *Science* magazine, Handkerchief Pool is no longer accessible to visitors because such abuse of springs usually destroys them. Here visitors play with handkerchiefs for the camera in 1922. (YNP Archives.)

For at least 15 years after automobiles were admitted into Yellowstone, park employees and visitors fondly remembered the recent stagecoach era. Bus driver Ralph Bush Sr. took this photograph in 1923 of his fellow drivers standing on and around a pile of horseshoes—the melancholy reminder of a bygone era. (Ralph Bush collection.)

After automobiles entered Yellowstone, gas stations and auto supplies proliferated, but the bodies of old stagecoaches remained in view as a reminder of those times. Here such a coach quietly deteriorated at Mammoth alongside a storage shed that was used for Goodrich tires around 1917. (YNP Archives.)

The Yellowstone Park Transportation Company motorized the park in 1917 by purchasing over 100 seven- and eleven-passenger cars, which most people called "buses." Here the bus fleet is shown parked at the Mammoth bus yard around 1920 on the site of today's Spruce Dormitory. Vestiges of the yard remained in place as late as 1976. After a disastrous fire destroyed over 90 buses in 1925, the company purchased new ones. (YNP Archives.)

The Yellowstone Park Transportation Company's fleet—116 or 117 of the 1917-model buses—is lined up in the fall of 1920 for this photograph by Jack E. Haynes. The seven-passenger buses can be seen at the front of the line, while the other 100 buses were 11-passenger vehicles. (YNP Archives.)

In 1923, the Union Pacific Railroad launched a campaign to advertise its trains to West Yellowstone, Montana. Hiring artist Walter Oehrle to draw clever images using bears, the railroad produced posters, sometimes more than one a year, that whetted vacationers' appetites for travel. In this photograph, Oehrle works at his sketch pad in 1930 while an assistant coaxes a bear to stand up so that Oehrle can sketch it. (NPS, Harpers Ferry.)

All lined up for 1923

The first of around 90 Union Pacific Railroad "bear" advertisements for trips to Yellowstone appeared in 1923. Shown here, it promoted the idea that Yellowstone's bears had somehow been made ready for visitors to see them. Walter Oehrle was the artist for most of this series. His art style continued through 1954, and after that, only six more were made, ending the bear series in 1960. (YNP Archives.)

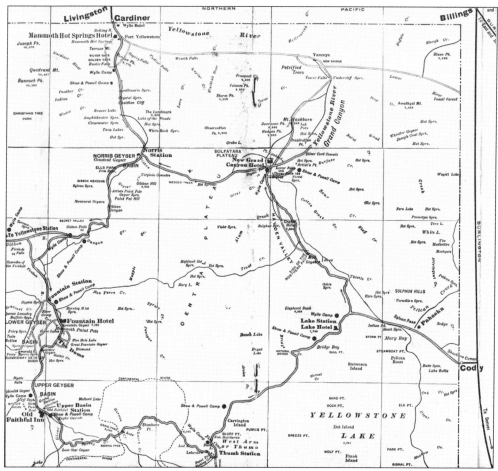

This map, published by the Chicago, Burlington, and Quincy Railroad in 1916, is rare and little known. Although somewhat distorted geographically, it is remarkable for the great number of old roads, cultural sites, and unusual natural features that it shows. Numerous Wylie Camping Company sites are noted, such as the Wylie Hotel at Gardiner and Wylie camps at Swan Lake Flats, Sleepy Hollow, Riverside, Upper Basin, West Thumb, Lake, and Canyon. The complete camps of Shaw and Powell Camping Company also appear. Natural features like Hygeia Spring, Wedded Trees, and "Sign of the Northern Pacific" are delineated. The 1880s Trout Creek road across the park's Central Plateau is shown, even though it had been out of use for 20 years by the time of this map. Likewise, the Crater Hills stage road through Hayden Valley is still shown, although it was falling out of use by 1916. The "old Norris Road," built in 1878, is shown, running from Amphitheater Springs to Norris Station to Artists' Paintpots to Gibbon Falls to Firehole River. Long-gone cultural features such as Fountain Station and Fountain Hotel appear here, but they would be gone within a few years. (Robert Goss collection.)

Corkscrew Bridge, on the park's east entrance road, was built as a wooden structure in 1904, after the road for stagecoaches was completed in 1903. It was a novel way for a primitive mountain road to gain elevation, and visitors saw it as such. The timber trestle was replaced by a shorter span in 1916. (YNP Archives.)

When automobiles were allowed into Yellowstone, it quickly became apparent that the old wooden Corkscrew Bridge would not hold the much heavier motor cars. Thus in 1919, the NPS built a new, concrete Corkscrew Bridge in the same place. By 1929, advances in technology made the bridge obsolete. A new road cut into the hillside above it bypassed the bridge, although observant motorists today can still look down and see the remnants of it. (YNP Archives.)

After motorization in 1917, Yellowstone Park Transportation Company decided that it needed buses in Cody, Wyoming. For around 20 years, the company had "Cody drivers" traveling from Cody to Canyon and back as a part of "loop" touring. Here, around 1929, the buses at Cody are, as was the custom, perfectly lined up when not in use. (Whittlesey collection.)

Ralph Bush and his friend Gary Cooper, who became a Hollywood movie star in 1925, went to Yellowstone from Butte, Montana, in 1923 to be bus drivers. Ralph left his photograph collection to his son Ralph Jr., and it influenced Ralph Jr. to work at Canyon Lodge in the early 1950s. Here drivers, including Gary Cooper (fourth row, left) pilot a YPT bus in a photograph that Ralph took in 1923 or 1924. (Ralph Bush Jr. collection.)

In this photograph, which Ralph Bush was especially proud of, driver Gary Cooper stands at far left at the highest point, while Ralph stands at bottom, second from right. They and their fellow bus drivers are posing behind Lake Hotel with a YPTC bus in 1923. (Ralph Bush Jr. collection.)

According to Ralph Bush Jr., after the 1924 season, Gary Cooper told Ralph Sr. that he was headed to California to see whether he could "get into the movies out there." Cooper's first movie, in 1925, was titled *The Thundering Herd* and was partly filmed in Yellowstone. Shown here is a scene from that movie, which captured Native Americans chasing buffalo. Park superintendent Horace Albright endured much criticism for allowing the stampeding and chasing of park bison. (NPS, Harpers Ferry.)

The view from the summit of Mount Washburn has been a celebrated one since 1870. Here VIPs touring the park in 1916 pose for a photograph before the lookout building was constructed. Included are army superintendent Lloyd Brett (fourth from left), director of the new National Park Service Stephen Mather (fifth from left), and his assistant Horace Albright (second from right). (YNP Archives.)

In January 1915, Stephen Mather spearheaded a campaign to establish the National Park Service. Mather and assistant Horace Albright went all out to cultivate the favor of influential people as well as the general public, and on August 15, 1916, Woodrow Wilson signed the NPS Act into law. Mather, the first director of the National Park Service, is pictured here on horseback near Hellroaring Peak in 1923. (YNP Archives.)

Built in 1921 at Gardiner, the north entrance checking station just inside the Roosevelt Arch was inconvenient in that rangers had to walk around an automobile to speak to its driver, and he was thus in the way of outbound traffic. The station burned on March 4, 1937, and a new one was built shortly after that, serving until it was razed in 1966. Today's log checking station was built in 1991. (YNP Archives.)

Two unidentified park rangers posed here on their motorcycles at Fort Yellowstone around 1924. The "cow pie" hat at left was unusual in that the NPS had that style for a relatively short time. (Martha Krueger collection.)

When the NPS was created, Yellowstone's rangers became more than protectors. Theirs was a mission that required a breadth of skills that included woodsman, teacher, conservationist, medic, firefighter, rescuer, wildlife manager, and role model for younger generations. The ranger became the face and voice of an agency designed to foster public affection for the national park. (YNP Archives.)

Replacing the U.S. Army as Yellowstone's protectors, the National Park Service took over existing soldier stations and also built additional ranger stations at various locations to more effectively manage and police the park. This unusual photograph of the new Madison Junction ranger station in front of National Park Mountain was taken around 1920. (YNP Archives.)

Horace Albright hired the first NPS "educational" ranger in Yellowstone in 1920. She was Isabel Bassett (Wasson), shown here a bit later and outside the park. Albright heard her giving a geological lecture to a tour group at Mammoth Hotel in 1919 and told her that if she would return the following year, he would hire her as a seasonal ranger. This he did, and she served as one of the first female "seasonals" in the NPS. (Peter Bergstrom collection.)

As the 1920s progressed, the National Park Service hired educational rangers to talk to visitors, and they were often noteworthy men with advanced degrees. As shown here, ranger naturalist Flottman lectures to a crowd of visitors at Doublet Pool in the Upper Geyser Basin about the scientific elements of Yellowstone's natural wonders as well as the importance of their conservation. (YNP Archives.)

This man was the first judge in Yellowstone. Robert Meldrum of Wyoming was appointed U.S. commissioner (judge) for Yellowstone in 1894 upon the passage of the Lacey Act, which protected park animals. Meldrum served until his death in 1936. Here he sits astride his horse in front of the stone house that was his home and office. Meldrum Mountain in the park was named for him. (YNP Archives.)

Two of Yellowstone's earliest explorers were represented at the 1922 fiftieth anniversary celebration of Yellowstone's founding. W. A. Hedges, a relative of Cornelius Hedges of the 1870 Washburn party, and Charles Cook, who led the 1869 Folsom party, were photographed with Supt. Horace Albright at the park's semi-centennial celebration. (YNP Archives.)

The dedication of Howard Eaton Trail at Sheepeater Cliff occurred on July 19, 1923. After Eaton's death in 1922, the trail was so christened. Sheepeater Cliff was selected because it had been Eaton's first campsite each year. Pictured at the dedication are, from left to right, Horace Albright (park superintendent), Stephen Mather (director of NPS), the two brothers of Howard Eaton, and Jack E. Haynes (park photographer). (YNP Archives.)

While stagecoaches disappeared in Yellowstone after 1916, the romance of the Old West nevertheless reemerged in the 1920s when large horse groups and hiking parties suddenly became chic. Shown here, one such horse party pauses for photographer Jack Haynes around 1925. (George Bowles collection.)

YELLOWSTONE PARK

TODD'S DELUXE PARTY

JULY 14 TO AUGUST 2nd 1924

TWENTY WONDERFUL DAYS

Frederick A. Todd
MANAGER
Box 217 Livingston Montana.

WEST COAST WINTER ADDRESS: P. O. DRAWER 769, STATION C., LOS ANGELES, CALIFORNIA

-: MAKE RESERVATIONS NOW!! - - PARTY LIMITED!! :-

This sign for Todd's Deluxe Tours advertised the idea of taking large horse parties to Yellowstone during a time (1924) when that had become stylish because of Howard Eaton's ever-growing horse parties and the dedication of the Howard Eaton Trail. In many ways, the 1920s were the heyday of large horse parties in Yellowstone. (YNP Archives.)

As shown here, the Yellowstone Park Transportation Company's horse rental operation at Old Faithful was located right in front of Old Faithful Inn during the 1920s. The company began running large pack trips to the backcountry after Howard Eaton's death in 1922, thus stimulating horse travel for the next decade or so. (YNP Archives.)

Pres. Calvin Coolidge visited Yellowstone in 1927. Here he, Superintendent Albright, and Secret Service men viewed Tower Fall from a platform. Amusingly, the sign there was "pluralized" by some well-meaning person who did not realize that the official name of the falls was "Tower Fall" (singular). (YNP Archives.)

Herbert Hoover visited Yellowstone while he was serving as secretary of commerce. He posed with Supt. Horace Albright and a freshly caught string of fish one day in 1928 and probably at Yellowstone Lake. (YNP Archives.)

## Seven

# DEPRESSION, INNOVATION, AND WAR

## 1930–1945

During the period 1930–1945, Yellowstone struggled with a lack of administrative money thanks to the decade-long Great Depression, fewer visitors because the American public had little money, and a looming world war that the United States joined in 1941. Park facilities and infrastructure deteriorated. Innovatively, Pres. Franklin Roosevelt's Civilian Conservation Corps entered Yellowstone to aid the beleaguered National Park Service.

The National Park Service continued its modernizing. It separated rangers into those who handled law enforcement duties and those who handled communications and interpretive duties. "Bear shows," wherein tourists watched bears eat hotel garbage poured onto platforms, continued to entertain visitors but added to administrative problems by encouraging those visitors to feed bears along roadsides. The Yellowstone Park Company was formed from the merger of six other independent companies. Workmen erected a new hotel at Mammoth Hot Springs and a large post office. Road crews began to pave park roads after years of maintaining them with only dirt, gravel, and oil. And rangers began to move toward using science and nature to manage park resources instead of allowing humans to manipulate them.

Biologists, geologists, fishery managers, and botanists were beginning to realize that natural areas like Yellowstone might be better off if humans manipulated them less. But as these debates became heated, scientists and managers were not quite sure that those innovations should be made and retreated to "we've-always-done-it-that-way" practices. While the NPS utilized World War II as an opportunity to abolish "bear feeding shows," other changes in resource management came slowly and were not completely implemented until the 1950s and 1960s.

The first Mammoth Hot Springs Hotel, built in 1883, had become ramshackle by 1913, so it was remodeled at that time into this building—the second Mammoth Hotel. The wing at right was also added in 1913. (YNP Archives.)

One of the old-style management decisions in Yellowstone was the long running practice of treating buffalo like cattle on a "ranch" in Lamar Valley. Perhaps "necessary" in 1902 to get the herd numbers up, the practice became increasingly dangerous, cumbersome, and unnatural as bison were moved to Mammoth from Lamar each year so that the public could view them in pens. Here 1920s visitors viewed the "tame herd" at a fenced area south of Mammoth. (YNP Archives.)

By the time of this 1930 photograph, the NPS had established hikes, lectures, information desks, and museums as its educational program. This sign advertised those services at Old Faithful. (YNP Archives.)

During the period 1926 to 1941, bear feeding shows were staged at Old Faithful and Canyon. Crowds watching the concrete platform at Canyon's Otter Creek (here around 1940) saw grizzly bears on it each night during the summer, all eating garbage dumped there by the National Park Service. Seagulls, ravens, magpies, and black bears waited for their turn at the food as well. Such shows ended after the 1941 season. (Montana Historical Society.)

The bear feeding show at Old Faithful utilized this wooden platform and sign. The show "is one of the most interesting features of the park to the majority of tourists," wrote Superintendent Albright, "but it requires careful regulation." Indeed, such regulation became dangerous and cumbersome. Bear feeding shows, popular from 1926 to 1941, were eventually abandoned because of growing disapproval among the scientific and conservation communities of the unnatural display of garbage-feeding bears. (YNP Archives.)

As shown here in 1939, the interior of the Hamilton swimming pool at Old Faithful was visually compatible with other architecture in the area. A pipeline from Solitary Geyser above Geyser Hill supplied water to the pool. (Montana Historical Society.)

Still in their heyday at the time of this photograph in 1930, Northern Pacific Railroad trains continued to bring visitors to the north entrance of Yellowstone through 1948. After that, the railroad ran "savage specials," trains that brought employees to the park as late as 1957. Thereafter, trains to Gardiner carried freight only through 1975, and Burlington Northern removed the tracks from Gardiner to Livingston in 1976. (YNP Archives.)

This humorous photograph, taken in 1932 at the Old Faithful garbage dump, illustrated what was then laughingly called the "rangers' Christmas tree." It was made from chamber pots, those metal containers that visitors to the Yellowstone camps used for overnight bathroom breaks. The man is unidentified. (NPS, Harpers Ferry.)

Gerald R. Ford, later president of the United States, served as a Yellowstone ranger during the summer of 1936. He autographed this photograph for the park collection and gave an oral history interview about his Yellowstone experiences to author Lee Whittlesey in 2000. That CD now resides in the park's collection. (YNP Archives.)

To National Park Service Rangers from a former ranger. Gerald R. Ford

The federal Volstead Act of 1919 inaugurated the prohibition of drinking alcohol in America. The law was a monstrous failure and was repealed in 1933, but during its tenure, federal officials enforced the act in Yellowstone. Here rangers pour out illegal, confiscated liquor at Mammoth in 1930 near Judge Meldrum's house. (YNP Archives.)

This photograph documented the ski house and skiers at Undine ski hill in February 1942, the year the park's small downhill ski area was established near Undine Falls. The Undine ski hill was open to the public but was used primarily to teach Mammoth schoolchildren how to ski. It was dismantled in the winter of 1993–1994. (YNP Archives.)

As shown here, Supt. Roger Toll's NPS car was stuck in deep snow on Dunraven Pass in 1933. Such photographs with gargantuan snow drifts have fascinated observers for at least 120 years because of the sheer amount of snow that accumulates in the park in winter. (YNP Archives.)

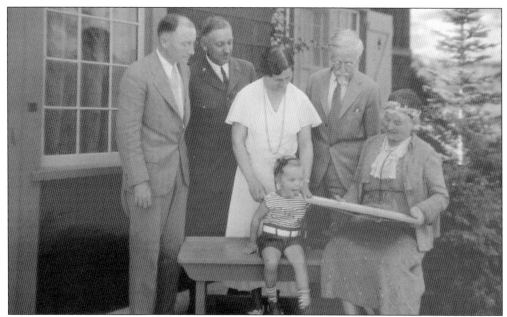

Historic Yellowstone personages gathered at Mammoth Hot Springs in front of photographer Jack Haynes's house in 1934. Pictured here from left to right are Montana historian Merrill Burlingame, chief naturalist Clyde Max Bauer, Isabel Haynes (Jack's wife), their daughter Lida Haynes, photographer William Henry Jackson, and Mary Hunter Doane (wife of Lt. Gustavus Doane of the 1870 Washburn Expedition). Mary Doane is probably holding a large, framed photograph of the new (1934) U.S. postage stamp of Old Faithful Geyser. (YNP Archives.)

Historic Yellowstone personages gathered at the Smithsonian Institute on March 12, 1927, shortly after artist Thomas Moran's death, in front of Moran's monumental painting *Grand Canyon of the Yellowstone*. From left to right are photographer William Henry Jackson, George B. Chittenden, S. B. Ladd, and William Henry Holmes. Interestingly, all had mountain peaks named after them, including Moran, and all had been associated with the 1870s Hayden surveys. (YNP Archives.)

Pres. Franklin Delano Roosevelt visited Yellowstone in 1937. Here he, Supt. Edmund Rogers, and Eleanor Roosevelt go touring. (YNP Archives.)

The Civilian Conservation Corps, established by Pres. Franklin Roosevelt, performed labor in Yellowstone to help the National Park Service during the period 1933–1941. Here four CCC enrollees, wearing official uniforms, take time off from their duties to examine the cone of Giant Geyser near Old Faithful. Standing on formations is prohibited today. (CCC.)

A Yellowstone Park Transportation Company bus driver in Bus No. 396 stops to allow his visitors to see Grotto Geyser, near Old Faithful, around 1936. Sadly, touring by bus fell out of favor after World War II, and the fleet was eventually sold. After an absence of over 40 years, several of these White touring buses were purchased by Xanterra Parks and Resorts, retrofitted to accommodate present automobile safety standards, and made a momentous return to Yellowstone in 2007. (YNP Archives.)

William Adams, a well-known conservationist, was photographed with his family at the "House of Horns" in 1930. This structure made of elk antlers was located in front of today's Horace Albright Museum at Mammoth Hot Springs during the period 1927 to 1963. Built by Chief Ranger Samuel Woodring, it was finally removed so as to no longer give visitors the impression that it was okay to collect elk antlers in the park. (YNP Archives.)

# *Eight*

# PROSPERITY AND ECOLOGICAL REGULATION
## 1946–1968

Rationing-sick and war-weary, Americans flocked to Yellowstone and other parks in huge numbers after World War II. For the first time, annual visitation topped one million in 1948. Fifteen years of depression and war had caused park buildings and infrastructure to seriously deteriorate. The National Park Service slowly instituted a 10-year program (1956–1966) called Mission 66 to upgrade such facilities in Yellowstone and other parks. While this program has not fared well under the subsequent scrutiny of historians, it arguably was the best that the service and the nation could afford during this period.

At the same time, the NPS began to look seriously at emerging science as a solution to many of its older resource management problems. Perhaps animal numbers did not need to be artificially controlled and fish artificially stocked in streams and lakes. Perhaps animals did not need to be fed by humans and hot springs tapped for heat and bathing. Perhaps bison did not need to be managed like cattle anymore. Perhaps humans no longer needed to kill predators. Looming largest of all was the park's 80-year-old bear problem: humans watched bears eat garbage in landfills called dumps and fed them along roadsides. This caused massive traffic jams and was unhealthy for bears. Resulting bear-human confrontations often culminated in rangers killing bears, a practice that no one liked.

In 1963, American scientists issued the "Leopold Report." A landmark for management of national parks, it stated that such areas should be kept as natural as possible with as little manipulation by humans as possible. Initially the NPS was slow to accept the recommendation, but the agency began to move on it in 1968. That year, NPS officials installed the first "bear-proof" trash cans in Yellowstone and instituted a program of closing open-pit garbage dumps and moving "troublesome" bears to the backcountry. By 1973, bears were no longer being fed by humans along park roadsides and were successfully being weaned from their long, artificial, human-food diets.

The NPS's transition from manipulating park resources to keeping them natural signaled the end of one philosophical period—that of manipulating park resources—and the beginnings of another—that of keeping parks natural, in what has been called "ecological process management."

Beginning in 1946, visitors came to Yellowstone in large numbers in their own cars. While buses have continued to carry some visitors to the present time, the bus era was largely over after the 1930s. Prosperity brought crowding in the park, and parking at Mammoth's Liberty Cap had clearly become crowded by the time of this *c.* 1955 photograph. (YNP Archives.)

Prior to 1957, "Canyon Village" was located at the present brink-of-Upper-Falls parking area and was referred to only as "Canyon." Here (around 1950) one can see a portion of the large Hamilton General Store at left and the gas station at right. The location today is empty and is reverting to wilderness. (YNP Archives.)

Fishing Bridge Village in the 1950s was a very developed area, with large numbers of rental cabins (right) and a large campground (top left). It arguably should never have been built because of its location in prime grizzly bear habitat. An extended fight with the town of Cody, Wyoming, whose officials did not want the village closed, ended with nature defeating development, and the village was largely demolished in the 1990s. (YNP Archives.)

Fishing Bridge itself, built in 1937 and shown here in 1951, became so crowded with fishermen standing elbow to elbow that it was permanently closed to fishing in 1974. Prior to that time, the river's critical function as a spawning area for native cutthroat trout was not well understood. (YNP Archives.)

Bears continued begging for food from park motorists through the summer of 1972. Here three black bears looked for a handout in 1958. Bear panhandling was one of the park's most difficult problems, not being completely solved until 1973. Feeding of bears is prohibited today. (NPS, Harpers Ferry.)

The NPS installed the first "bear-proof" trash cans in 1968 (shown here) and 1969. A 50-pound metal lid attached to a pole that was sunk into a 400-pound (buried) concrete block kept odors mostly inside the can, and odors were what attracted bears. Although a determined bear could get into the can if it tried hard enough, most bears were discouraged enough that the park's open-garbage-can problem was solved. (YNP Archives.)

The third Canyon Hotel (1911–1958) was a huge affair, more than a mile in circumference. As this 1941 aerial photograph showed, the hotel was strangely shaped but beloved by nearly everyone who stayed there or worked there. Closed after the 1958 season because of foundational problems, it was sold to a wrecking company and accidentally burned to the ground during demolition in August 1960. (YNP Archives.)

The third Canyon Hotel burned on the night of August 8, 1960. No one knows how the fire started, but it has been postulated that it began from a burning candle. Employees were known to have been using the closed building as a party site, and perhaps one of them inadvertently started the fire. (YNP Archives.)

The Yellowstone earthquake of August 17, 1959, measured 7.5 on the Richter scale and was one of the strongest earthquakes ever recorded on earth. Damage to stone buildings at Mammoth meant that the park superintendent and other officials were housed for a short time in tents. This was the superintendent's tent at that time. From left to right are Dave Beal, Lee Coleman, Huntley Child Jr., Supt. Lon A. Garrison, John Q. Nichols, Luis Gastellum, Garfield N. Helppie, Jack E. Haynes, Joseph Joffe, and Tom Hyde. (YNP Archives.)

The park's 1959 earthquake caused big changes in geysers and hot springs, drying up some, causing others to erupt, and in some cases actually starting new springs. Red Spouter Geyser at Lower Geyser Basin, shown here that year or soon after, had its origins in the earthquake. The geyser spouted red, muddy water. (YNP Archives.)

Snow planes appeared in Yellowstone long before there was a formal winter season. Indeed Walt Stuart built the first known snow plane at West Yellowstone about 1935. They could go very fast over snow, but their rear propellers at ground level made them potentially dangerous. Nevertheless, these machines took some visitors into Old Faithful during winters in the late 1940s. Replaced by snowcoaches in the 1950s, snow planes quietly disappeared. (Whittlesey collection from Walt Stuart.)

Snowcoaches made their appearance in Yellowstone in the winter of 1954–1955, when Harold Young and Billy Nichols of West Yellowstone purchased a few from Bombardier and got permission to run them into Old Faithful. They sold out to Yellowstone Park Company in 1967, and many of those same snowcoaches, their parts changed many times, still run today. (YNP Archives.)

Old Faithful Geyser long ago became synonymous with Yellowstone Park. Even today tourists are heard to say, "How do I get to Yellowstone? I mean Old Faithful." So famous is this geyser that some visitors think it is the only one in the park, and most think that it is the biggest, the tallest, the hottest, the most regular, has the greatest water discharge, and so on, when in fact it is none of those. But it certainly is the most famous geyser. Because of its complex history, Old Faithful Geyser has become, through time, almost as much a cultural feature as a natural feature. (Bob Barry Collection/ YNP Archives.)

# INDEX

# DISCOVER THOUSANDS OF LOCAL HISTORY BOOKS FEATURING MILLIONS OF VINTAGE IMAGES

Arcadia Publishing, the leading local history publisher in the United States, is committed to making history accessible and meaningful through publishing books that celebrate and preserve the heritage of America's people and places.

Find more books like this at
**www.arcadiapublishing.com**

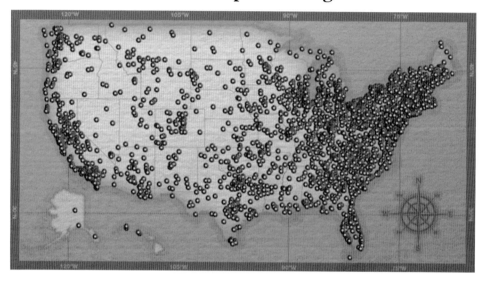

Search for your hometown history, your old stomping grounds, and even your favorite sports team.